Picture the Past
Life in
New Amsterdam

Laura Fischer

Heinemann Library
Chicago, Illinois

Produced for Heinemann Library by
  Bender Richardson White.
Editor: Lionel Bender
Designer and Media Conversion: Ben White
Picture Researcher: Cathy Stastny
Production Controller: Kim Richardson

07 06 05 04 03
10 9 8 7 6 5 4 3 2 1

Printed and bound by Lake Book Manufacturing, Inc.

Library of Congress Cataloging-in-Publication Data.
Fischer, Laura, 1977-
  Life in New Amsterdam / Laura Fischer.
    p. cm. -- (Picture the past)
  Summary: An overview of life from 1624 to 1664 in New Amsterdam, a Dutch colony which was the first settlement along the Hudson River Valley in New York state and which grew to be New York City.
  Includes bibliographical references (p.) and index.
  ISBN 1-4034-3798-X -- ISBN 1-4034-4285-1 (pbk.)
  1. New York (N.Y.)--History--Colonial period, ca. 1600-1775--Juvenile literature. 2. New York (N.Y.)--Social life and customs--To 1775--Juvenile literature. (1. New York (N.Y.)--History--Colonial period, ca. 1600-1775. 2. New York (N.Y.)--Social life and customs--To 1775.) I. Title. II. Series.
  F128.4.F57 2003
  947.7'103--dc21
                                        2003005418

Special thanks to Angela McHaney Brown at Heinemann Library for editorial and design guidance and direction.

Acknowledgments
The producers and publishers are grateful to the following for permission to reproduce copyright material:
Corbis Images: Bettmann Archives, p. 13; David Zimmerman, p. 30; Collection of The New-York Historical Society, New York, U.S.A., p. 23. North Wind Pictures, cover and pp. 3, 6, 12, 14, 15, 16, 19, 22, 26, 27. The Bridgeman Art Library: British Library, London, U.K., page 9; David Findlay Jr. Fine Art, N.Y.C., U.S.A., p. 18; Hamburg Kunsthalle, Hamburg, Germany, p. 28; Museum of the City of New York, U.S.A., pp. 1, 7; Collection of The New-York Historical Society, New York, U.S.A., pp. 11, 17, 25. Private collections, pp. 21, 24.

Maps: Stefan Chabluk
Illustrations: James Field, p. 20; Nick Hewetson, p. 8; John James, pp. 4, 10, 29.

Every effort has been made to contact copyright holders of any material reproduced in this book. Omissions will be rectified in subsequent printings if notice is given to the publisher.

ABOUT THIS BOOK

This book describes what life was like from 1624 to 1664 in New Amsterdam, a part of the **colony** of New Netherland. This colony was first settled along the Hudson River Valley in what is now New York state. Soon after New Netherland was set up, it became centered in New Amsterdam, what is today the island of Manhattan in New York City. New Amsterdam was named for the city of Amsterdam in the Netherlands, from which many of **colonists** had come. As well as **Dutch** colonists, people from other countries in Western Europe, and from the Caribbean and west Africa, also lived in the colony.

We have illustrated this book with paintings and drawings from colonial times and with artists' ideas of how things looked then.

The Author

Laura Fischer is a professional writer and editor residing in Chicago, Illinois. She has worked with a variety of online, magazine, and book publishers, and has a special interest in children's literature and nonfiction. She graduated from Michigan State University with a B.A. in English, and is currently working toward an M.A. in elementary education at DePaul University.

Note to the Reader

Some words are shown in bold, **like this.** You can find out what they mean by looking in the glossary.

CONTENTS

New Colonies

For thousands of years, **Native Americans** were the only people to live in the land we call North America. Beginning in the late 1440s, European leaders decided to send people to explore this land. Countries such as Spain, England, France, and the Netherlands sent ships full of people and supplies across the Atlantic Ocean to the **New World.** At first, the people came to trade goods with the Native Americans and then return to their homeland. Later, people came to create **colonies** for their home country.

Look for these

The illustration of a New Amsterdam boy and girl shows you the subject of each double-page story in the book.

The illustration of a windmill marks boxes with interesting facts about life in New Amsterdam.

TIMELINE OF EVENTS IN NEW AMSTERDAM, 1624–1664

1609 Henry Hudson explores what is now the Hudson River

1621 The **Dutch** West India Company is created to help set up Dutch colonies

1624 New Netherland is founded in what is now the states of New York, New Jersey, and Connecticut

1600   1610   1620   1630   1635

1626 The town of New Amsterdam is founded

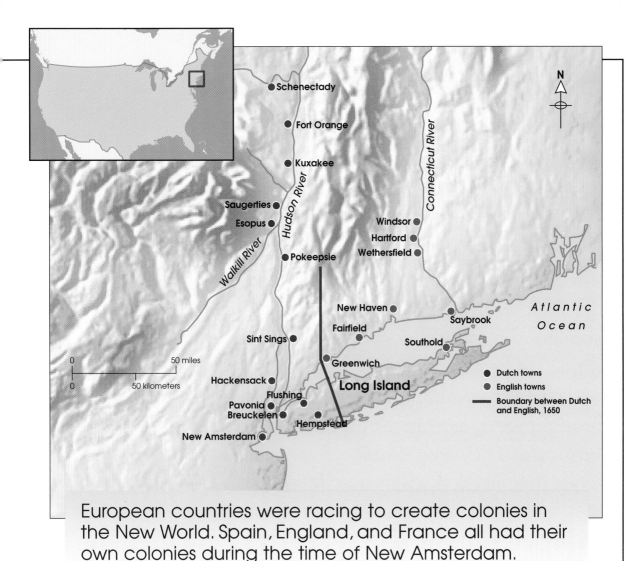

European countries were racing to create colonies in the New World. Spain, England, and France all had their own colonies during the time of New Amsterdam.

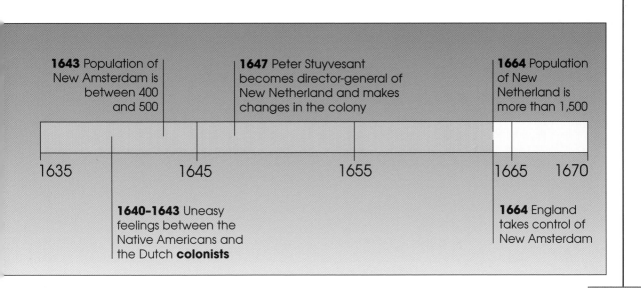

1643 Population of New Amsterdam is between 400 and 500

1647 Peter Stuyvesant becomes director-general of New Netherland and makes changes in the colony

1664 Population of New Netherland is more than 1,500

1635   1645   1655   1665   1670

1640–1643 Uneasy feelings between the Native Americans and the Dutch **colonists**

1664 England takes control of New Amsterdam

Making the Trip

To get to the **New World,** the **Dutch settlers** traveled by sailing ships across the Atlantic Ocean. The journey was uncomfortable and took two months. The ships carried people and all the supplies they would need when they landed. The **colonists** brought tools with them to build homes. They also brought food, clothing, and a little furniture. They would make the rest of what they needed when they landed.

SHIP'S DOCTOR

Two "comforters of the sick" traveled on the ships with the colonists to help them when they became ill. They were like doctors, but they did not have the modern medicine and supplies that doctors today have. Often, they just prayed with their patients.

The supplies and people from oceangoing ships were unloaded onto smaller boats, which then brought them to shore.

At first only men came over. They traded with the **Native Americans** and sent valuable beaver skins and furs back to the Netherlands on boats. The traders formed small settlements, where they lived and traded. Then, in 1624, whole families traveled to the new Dutch **colony.** Thirty families traveled together on one ship.

This is a view of New Amsterdam in about 1653. The families of New Amsterdam settled close to the shore. They drank and washed in fresh water from the Hudson River.

Creating a Town

The **colonists** of New Amsterdam created a town from the wilderness. They cut down trees and used the wood and bark to make houses. Early on, the **settlers** built a **fort** with earth and stone walls, and **canons** for protection. The colonists built their houses in neat rows, surrounding Fort Amsterdam. Dirt roads ran between the lines of houses.

The land of New Amsterdam had much to offer the colonists. They built houses with wood from local trees on rich land that was good for farming.

Beyond the houses, the colonists planted gardens and farm fields for everyone to use and share. Later, ships full of cows, pigs, horses, and sheep were sent over from the Netherlands. Large **pastures** were cleared out of the woods for the animals to graze on.

In this map, you can see Fort Amsterdam (on the right), the colonists' houses (in the center), and the gardens and pastures (on the left).

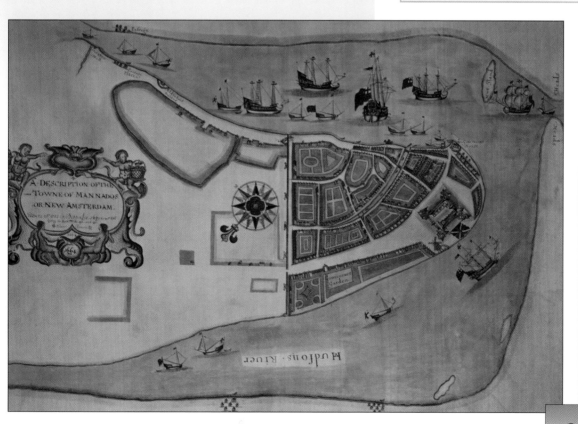

New Neighbors

Native Americans from the Iroquois, Huron, and Algonquin tribes had lived on the land for thousands of years before the **Dutch colonists** arrived. The Native Americans hunted foxes, beavers, and rabbits. They traded the furs to the Dutch, who used them for making hats and fur collars. In exchange, the Native Americans received cloth, blankets, and tools made of metal, such as knives.

The Algonquins who lived in the area were skilled hunters and fishermen. They also grew many types of **crops,** including corn, squash, and tobacco.

The colonists and Native Americans were friendly with one another. Some Dutch colonists even married Native Americans and started families.

Generally, the Native Americans and colonists got along well. But one time a colonial governor tried to make the Native Americans pay a **tax.** They did not think they should have to pay the tax. They **revolted,** and the fighting lasted for almost seven years. People on both sides died. After the fighting, a peace agreement was made.

WALL STREET

The name of Wall Street in New York City comes from the time of the Dutch colonists. Today's Wall Street is in the same place as a wall that they built to protect themselves from attacks by Native Americans.

Protecting the Town

Fort Amsterdam was the center of life in New Amsterdam. **Canons** were placed on its walls to protect the **colony** from **settlers** from nearby English colonies who might want to attack the city. A wall was also built along the eastern part of the city to protect it. Safe behind the wall was the town hall. In **Dutch** the town hall was called the *stadt huys* (you say "stahdt hoose").

This illustration of the town shows:
A. the fort
B. the church
C. the **windmill**
D. the gallows, for hanging criminals
E. the town hall, courts, and jail
F. the director-general's house
G. gallows
H. the town square

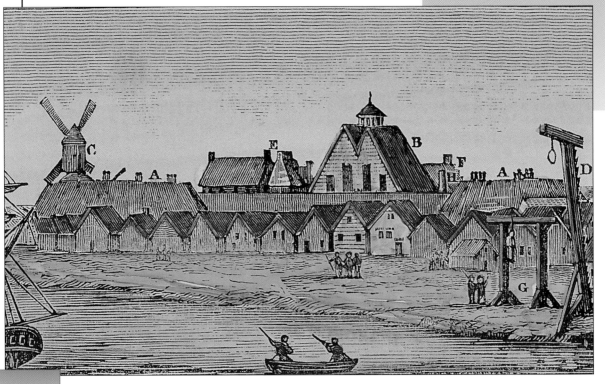

When news from the Netherlands arrived in the colony, a bell was rung in the town hall. All the colonists gathered inside, where the news was read out loud to them. The news was then posted on the walls of the building for the people who knew how to read. In those days, not everyone knew how to read.

Meetings in the town hall allowed **colonists** to express their opinions and make decisions for the colony. Here, director-general Peter Stuyvesant argues with colonial leaders about laws and **taxes.**

Houses

The early houses of New Amsterdam were made of wood and bark with **thatched** roofs. Later, houses were built with bricks and tiles sent over from the Netherlands. The **colonists** wanted to make their buildings look like the buildings of their homeland.

FIRE

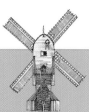

Sometimes a spark from the fireplace would set a house's chimney on fire. The fire would then spread to the thatched roof. To fight fires, colonists placed leather buckets filled with water around the colony. When a house caught fire, the colonists would line up and pass the buckets from person to person to throw water on the fire.

Like houses today, Dutch houses were built in rows so that the front of each house faced the street.

The roofs of many houses went up in a stair-step pattern, just as buildings did in Amsterdam. Also to remind them of home, the colonists planted tulip bulbs from the Netherlands in flower beds around their houses. Often, housewives found loose pigs or sheep feeding or sleeping in their flower beds. The animals had roamed away from the **pastures.**

As in their homeland, the colonists built canals to allow boats and small ships to bring supplies into the town.

Inside a Home

Houses were heated by fireplaces. Families used the fireplace in the main room for heating the house and cooking food. Inside the main room was a large wooden dining table. Woven carpets and fabrics were draped over the table when it was not in use. At mealtimes, people sat down on benches or on wooden chairs with leather seats. Shelves on the walls held colorful pottery and china.

Families gathered near the fireplace because it was a source of warmth and light. Most homes had a foot stove. This would have been filled with hot coals from the fire and placed near a person's feet to keep them warm.

Floors were sometimes covered in fine white sand or straw to keep them dry. People slept on beds stuffed with feathers or straw. These beds were dusty and lumpy compared to today's mattresses. Colonial houses had no plumbing or electricity. The cool cellar of the house was used to store food.

THE KAS

Because **Dutch** houses did not have closets, each house had a large, wooden cabinet called a *kas* to store linen, blankets, and clothing. These cabinets were often painted with fancy decorations and passed down from parent to child.

A doctor helps a sick woman in her home. Straw covers the floor. Fabrics cover the tables. A door on the window could be closed to keep out drafts.

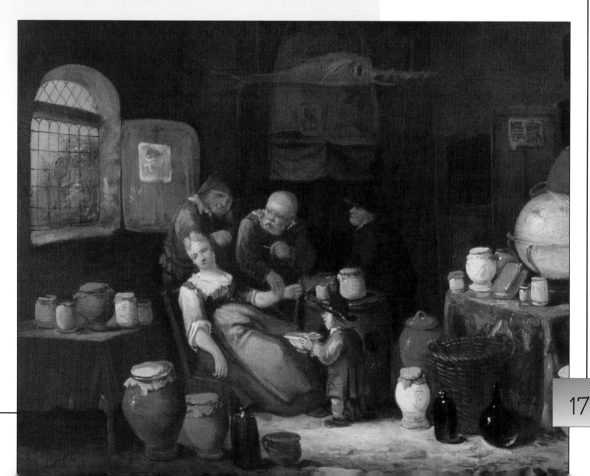

Farms

Colonists made one large area of the colony into farm fields, gardens, and pastures for the animals. The colonists grew all their own vegetables, grains, and other crops. Before they could use the land, though, they had to cut down all the trees. Then they used oxen to pull heavy plows through the fields to make the soil ready for planting seeds. Everyone shared this land together.

The land around the Hudson River was covered in trees. The colonists cut down many trees to clear land for farming. They also cut down trees for wood to build houses and furniture, and to burn in fireplaces.

The colonists grew wheat and corn to grind into flour for making bread. To grind the grain, the colonists used **windmills.** They brought the idea with them from the Netherlands. The windmills used the power of the wind to turn heavy round stones to grind grain. The colonists also planted apple, pear, and peach trees in **orchards.**

This is a farm and **blacksmith's** shop near the East River on Manhattan Island. The arms of the windmill caught the wind and turned. Windmills were used for pumping water, cutting wood, and grinding grain.

Daily Life

New Amsterdam was a busy place, especially at the harbor. Merchants brought goods to the harbor to be loaded onto ships sailing to the Netherlands.

Life was busy for the **colonists.** Men spent the day hunting, fishing, and trading with the **Native Americans.** They also worked hard to plan and build buildings, and to set up the town. Women worked at home. They cooked food, sewed clothing, cleaned the house, took care of animals, and tended the garden.

Children helped their mothers with the housework. Some children went to school. When they were not working, children found time for play. In the cold months they ice skated and rode down snowy hills on homemade sleds. In warm months they played ball or chasing games outside.

At an outdoor workshop, workers made wooden shoes called *klompen.* These were similar to modern clogs. The workers carved the shoes from tree trunks.

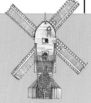

HAND-MADE

Almost everything a housewife used or needed was made by hand. Women made their own dyes for fabric, their own soap for washing, and their own brooms and brushes for cleaning. Using a spinning wheel, they spun sheep's wool into yarn. They wove the yarn into fabric from which they made clothes.

21

School

Families in New Amsterdam had to pay for their children to go to school. Children from poor families could not afford school. Students of all ages learned together in the same room. They studied religion, reading, and writing. Girls went home in the afternoon, while boys stayed in school a couple hours longer to learn arithmetic.

Young children did not go to school. They stayed at home and played. Children of all ages were taught by their parents to help with jobs in the house.

In school, each child had a hornbook. This was a flat piece of wood with a cover of animal horn made clear by putting it in boiling water. Papers to read were placed under the cover to protect them.

There was one male teacher for all the students. Students were expected to sit still and be quiet and well behaved. If they misbehaved, the teacher could punish them. In church on Sunday, the students would chant out loud what they had learned in school during the week. The whole **colony** would listen to them.

Clothing and Shoes

Women in New Amsterdam wore long, full skirts of dark colors and white blouses that laced up the front. They wore dark vests or close-fitting short jackets over their blouses. They fastened wide collars made of white linen over their jackets. Wealthier **colonists** wore collars and bonnets trimmed with homemade lace.

WOODEN SHOES

Colonists wore *klompen* when they worked in the fields. These wooden shoes could be scraped clean, and they protected the colonists' feet. In cold weather, they stuffed the shoes with hay for extra warmth.

Colonists' clothes were made of linen, which they wore in the summer, or wool, to keep them warm in the winter. In town, people wore leather shoes.

Men dressed in pants called breeches
that were tight up to the knee and
baggy above the knee. They wore
button-up jackets of dark colors and
hats with wide brims. They wore white
collars outside of their jackets. Boys and
girls dressed the same as grown-ups.

This is a portrait
of the son of
a leader of
the **colony** of
New Amsterdam.
He is dressed in
the finest clothes
of the time.

25

What Colonists Ate

The **colonists** grew all their own food. There were no stores where they could buy supplies. The colonists planted fields with wheat and corn and made breads, cookies, cakes, pretzels, and waffles from the flour. They grew beans, squash, pumpkins, and potatoes in vegetable gardens. They also raised pigs and cows and hunted wild animals such as turkey, goose, duck, and deer.

Families ate meals together at a big table. Because they lived near the shore, the colonists ate a lot of fresh fish, lobsters, and oysters. For fruit, they ate apples, peaches, and pears from their orchards.

Meat and fish were packed in salt to preserve them. This made them last through the winter months, when fresh food was hard to get. The colonists also pickled vegetables and fish to make them last. They did this by soaking the foods in vinegar. Women made their own cheese and butter from cow's milk, just as they did in the Netherlands. Women also turned fruit into sweet jams.

Wealthy people could afford to buy fancy foods from Europe, such as tea, coffee, chocolate, and raisins. Here, a family is drinking tea.

Cooking Food

The **colonists** baked bread and pies in a shared bakehouse with help from a baker. At home, they cooked food in a big fireplace. They prepared many foods in a **Dutch** oven, which was a heavy iron pot with a lid. The Dutch oven sat over the coals of the fire with more hot coals resting on the lid. This way, it could cook foods from the top and the bottom.

Cooks hung heavy pots of stews and soups from hooks over the fire. They roasted big pieces of meat in the fire.

Colonial Dutch Recipe—Pancakes

The Dutch colonists made many types of pancakes and waffles. *Pannekoeken*—very thin pancakes—were served for breakfast or as a dessert.

WARNING: Do not cook anything unless there is an adult to help you. Always ask an adult to help you use the oven and to handle hot foods.

FOLLOW THE STEPS

1. In a large bowl, beat the eggs. Add the sugar, baking powder, and salt. Mix in half the milk and half the flour. Stir to combine. Stir in the rest of the milk and flour until the mixture is smooth and thin.

2. Heat a large nonstick frying pan over medium heat. Melt a half teaspoon of butter in the pan. To make the pancakes, pour about 1/3 cup of batter into the pan. Tilt the pan to spread the batter out evenly and thinly. Cook one minute or until the edges of the pancake turn brown. Flip the pancake and cook for 30 more seconds.

3. Stack the pancakes on a plate. When all pancakes are cooked, spread each pancake with a thin layer of butter. Sprinkle each pancake with cinnamon and sugar, roll them up, and serve.

Becoming New York

In 1664, England took control of the **colony** of New Netherland, which included New Amsterdam. The new English colony was renamed New York. The colony of New York became a state when the colonies broke away from England in 1776 to form the United States. What was once New Amsterdam grew to become the busy city we call New York City.

In New York City today, skyscrapers and office buildings line the streets where New Amsterdam houses once stood.

NEW YORK NAMES

Many names of streets and areas in modern New York are taken from names the **Dutch colonists** used.

Then:	**Now:**
Haarlem	Harlem
Breukelen	Brooklyn
Bowerie	Bowery
Jonker	Yonkers

Glossary

blacksmith person who makes tools and other things from iron

canon large gun that fires heavy metal balls

colony new village, town, or area that is set up by a country in a new or different land. The people are known as *colonists.*

crop plants that are grown in large amounts for using or selling

Dutch people or items from the Netherlands

fort building that is protected with walls and weapons to defend a city

Native American member of one of the first groups of people to live in North and South America

New World the continents of North and South America

orchard group of fruit trees

ox strong animal, similar to a big cow, that is used for work. More than one ox are called oxen.

pasture large field of grass used as food by grazing animals

plow farming tool used to cut up and loosen soil

quill large, stiff feather with a hollow end and used for writing

revolt to disagree with someone and fight against them

settler person who makes a new home in a new place

tax money people must pay to the government for items bought or owned

thatched covered with layers of straw or hay

windmill structure that uses wind power to grind grain into flour

---

More Books to Read

Davis, Kevin A. *Look What Came from the Netherlands.* Danbury, Conn.: Franklin Watts, 2002.

Krizner, L.J. *Peter Stuyvesant: New Amsterdam and the Origins of New York.* New York: Rosen, 2001.

Lilly, Melinda. *The Dutch in New Amsterdam.* Vero Beach, Fla.: Rourke, 2002

Index